GREATEST WARRIORS
ROMAN SOLDIERS

PETER HEPPLEWHITE

ARCTURUS

This edition first published in 2014 by Arcturus Publishing

Distributed by Black Rabbit Books
P.O. Box 3263
Mankato
Minnesota MN 56002

Edited and designed by: Discovery Books Ltd.

Library of Congress Cataloging-in-Publication Data

Hepplewhite, Peter.
 Roman soldiers / Peter Hepplewhite.
    p cm. -- (Greatest warriors)
 Includes index.
 Summary: "Provides readers with exciting details, facts, and statistics about historical Roman soldiers"--Provided by publisher.
 Audience: Grades 4-6.
 ISBN 978-1-78212-402-3 (library binding)
 1. Rome--Army--Juvenile literature. 2. Rome--Army--Military life--Juvenile literature. I. Title.
 U35.H47 2014
 355.00937--dc23
                        2013005690

Series concept: Joe Harris
Managing editor for Discovery Books: Laura Durman
Editor: Clare Collinson
Picture researcher: Clare Collinson
Designer: Ian Winton

The publisher would like to thank the following re-enactment groups for their assistance in the preparation of this book: Britannia (www.durolitum.co.uk/) and Ermine Street Guard (http://www.erminestreetguard.co.uk/).

Picture credits:
Alamy: pp. 4, 28 (Photos 12), p. 7 (INTERFOTO), pp. 14, 15, 16 (Stephen Mulcahey), p. 18 (Jeff Morgan 16), p. 26 (AF archive), p. 27 (Martin Jenkinson); Britannia (www.durolitum.co.uk/): p. 22; Ermine Street Guard: pp. 9, 19tr; Getty Images: p. 6 (Celia Paterson), p. 21 (Gamma-Rapho), p. 23 (uplifted); Shutterstock Images: p. 10l (greglith), p. 10r (Rolandino), p. 17 (Regien Paassen), p. 24 (McCarthy's PhotoWorks), p. 29 (StockPhotoAstur); Wikimedia Commons: pp. title, 5, 11l, 11r, 12, 19bl, 25 (MatthiasKabel), p. 8 (Luc Viatour), p. 13, p. 20 (Portable Antiquities Scheme).
Cover images: Shutterstock Images: top (SueC), bottom center (meunierd), background (Francisco Javier Gil).

Printed in China

SL002668US
Supplier 03, Date 0513, Print Run 2359

CONTENTS

IMPERIAL ARMY

The Roman army was the greatest fighting force in the ancient world. It conquered and defended a vast **empire** that lasted for over 500 years (27 BCE–476 CE). Roman warriors were highly trained, tightly disciplined, and well armed. Battle **tactics**, practiced over and over again, made Roman soldiers very hard to beat.

SUPREME WARRIORS

The most important soldiers in the Roman army were infantry, or foot soldiers. They served in units called legions, each with around 5,000 men.

A PROFESSIONAL ARMY

By the first century CE, Rome's empire covered most of Europe, North Africa, and the Middle East. To conquer new lands and defend its **frontiers**, Rome built up a permanent army, made up of professional, full-time soldiers. Ruthless and highly skilled in battle, Roman **legionaries** were the most powerful and feared warriors of their time.

CAVALRY

Every legion had a small force of about 120 cavalry, or soldiers who fought on horseback.

COMBAT STATS

Empire and army, 117 CE

- **Population of Rome:** around 1 million
- **Population of the Roman Empire:** around 88 million
- **Size of Roman Empire:** 2.5 million square miles (6.5 million sq km)
- **Number of troops:** about 350,000 (legionaries and **auxiliaries**)
- **Long-lasting legion:** Third Cyrenean Legion—by 117 CE, it had already existed for over 150 years and continued to fight for another 350 years

CRACK TROOPS

Roman legionaries were the most disciplined and well-organized warriors the world had ever known. They received rigorous training and obeyed commands without question and without delay. On the battlefield, they fought as units, forming a fearsome war machine.

ROUTE MARCH

Legionaries were trained to march quickly. Three times a month, every legion underwent a grueling route march in full armor—22 miles (35 km) in 5 hours at a quick step.

CITIZEN ARMY

The legionaries in the **imperial** army were all Roman **citizens**—free men who could vote in elections. They were mainly volunteers who served 20 years as full-time soldiers, followed by five years as **reserves**. They received 225 *denarii* a year for their service and a pension of 3,000 *denarii* or a grant of land when they retired.

FIGHTING UNITS

The number of legions in the army varied, but it was usually around 30. Each soldier belonged to a squad called a *contubernia*, a group of eight men who shared a tent and ate together. Ten *contubernia* made up a **century**. Six centuries made up a **cohort**, and there were 10 cohorts in each legion.

MASTERS OF MOVEMENT
Roman legionaries were trained to maneuver with great precision and organization. The units formed a close-knit fighting force that seemed unstoppable.

COMBAT STATS
Imperial legions

- **Legions:** around 30 legions in the Roman army, each with about 5,000 men
- **Cohorts:** 10 cohorts in each legion; 9 cohorts with 480 men and 1 cohort with 800 men
- **Centuries:** 6 centuries of 80 men in each cohort, except the first cohort, which had 5 double-strength centuries of 160 men
- **Contubernia:** 10 *contubernia* of 8 men in each century

OFFICERS IN COMMAND

Roman legionaries were the supreme warriors of their day, but key to their success were the officers in charge. The commanding officer of each legion was the **legate**. He was handpicked by the **emperor** and usually a **noble** and a **senator**. But the **centurions** were the backbone of the army. They led the soldiers into battle.

TRANSVERSE CREST
A centurion's helmet had a large plumed crest running from ear to ear, so his men could see him in battle.

CENTURION
A centurion was the officer in charge of each century.

MILITARY MEDALS
Military awards or medals, called *phalerae*, were worn on the centurion's chest.

SPECIAL DUTIES

Second in command of each century was the *optio*. He helped to organize the troops and ensured that the centurion's orders were carried out. Each century also included officers with special duties.

VEXILLARIUS

The *vexillarius* was the officer who carried the flag of the legion, the *vexillum*.

OPTIO

The *optio's* badge of office was a decorated silver staff.

SIGNIFER

Each century had a **standard** bearer called a *signifer*. The standard bearer could pass on simple orders, such as "advance," by raising, lowering, or waving the standard.

CORNICEN

The trumpet blower, or *cornicen*, helped soldiers march in time and give signals to the troops. When battle noise drowned out the commands of officers, a trumpet blast meant "look at the standard and follow it." *Cornicens* wore a wolf skin as part of their uniform.

FIGHTING TALK

Verus—ambitious centurion

Verus was an able centurion who became a senator and commander of the Third Gallic Legion in Syria. But in 219 CE, he became too ambitious. He led his legion in a rebellion against Emperor Elagabalus and proclaimed himself emperor. As punishment, Verus was executed and the legion was broken up—a great disgrace.

EQUIPPED FOR CONQUEST

Roman soldiers were highly skilled with a variety of deadly weapons. A legionary's main armaments were his sword, shield, and javelin. He could also call on other weapons, such as daggers and darts, when the need arose.

JAVELIN

A legionary's javelin (*pilum*) was a 6.6-foot (2-m) long wooden shaft with a barbed iron tip for piercing armor. Javelins could be used in hand-to-hand combat but were usually thrown before engaging with the enemy. They had a maximum range of about 100 feet (30 m).

SWORD

A Roman legionary's most important weapon was his sword (*gladius*). This was made of double-edged steel, strengthened with carbon.

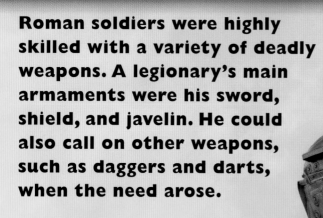

SHIELD

The curved, rectangular Roman shield was called a *scutum*. It was not just used for defense. In close combat, a legionary would ram his opponent with the shield, while thrusting with his sword.

A WARRIOR'S PACK

In early Roman times, mules were used to carry most of a legionary's equipment. But large baggage trains slowed armies down, so from the first century BCE, legionaries were expected to carry as much of their own equipment as they could. Each soldier also had to carry his share of the tools, such as spades, axes, and picks, that would be needed for building camps and fortifications at the end of the march.

HEAVY LOAD

As well as their own weapons and armor, Roman legionaries on the march had to carry a heavy supply pack on a wooden cross frame.

MARCHING PACK

A legionary's pack included between three and 15 days' worth of food supplies, as well as pans for cooking and a bedroll or cloak.

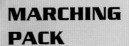

COMBAT STATS

Equipment stats
- **Length of sword:** 25-32 inches (64-81 cm)
- **Length of dagger:** 8-10 inches (20-25 cm)
- **Length of spear:** about 6.6 feet (2 m)
- **Total weight of equipment carried:** at least 60 pounds (27 kg)–about the weight of a husky dog!

DRESSED FOR WAR

Roman legionaries fought many vicious battles throughout the empire. To protect themselves from their enemies' weapons, they wore the best armor in the ancient world.

MAIL ARMOR

Chain mail armor was used throughout the Roman period. The mail was made by linking thousands of small iron rings together.

SHIELD

As well as body armor, a legionary had a shield for protection against enemy blows. Shaped to curve around the body, it was about 4 feet long (120 cm) and 2 feet (60 cm) wide. It weighed about 22 pounds (10 kg).

GREAVES

Leg armor called "greaves" gave protection from the knee to the ankle. In later times, only centurions wore greaves.

SANDALS

A legionary's sandals were designed to help him march for long distances. They were strong and well ventilated and often had metal studs on the soles to make them last longer.

PLATE ARMOR

Chain mail armor could withstand cuts from swords, but it did not give good protection from stabbing blows. From the first century CE, legionaries wore armor made of curved plates, called *lorica segmentata*. This gave excellent protection for the body and shoulders.

HELMET

Helmets of brass or iron protected the head. Hinged cheek plates were tied with leather straps under the chin. The helmets were designed to allow for good vision and hearing. A guard, sticking out from the back, protected the soldier's neck.

OVERLAPPING ARMOR

Lorica segmentata was body armor made from overlapping metal strips held together with hinges and leather straps. This not only gave the wearer protection, but also freedom of movement.

FIGHTING TALK

Uniform protection

Roman legionaries wore a standard uniform, depending on their unit. This meant items such as helmets or sandals could be made in large numbers to keep costs down. Soldiers had to pay for any lost or damaged items, so uniforms were usually well looked after.

BACKUP TROOPS

Roman legions were given vital support by auxiliaries. Auxiliaries were light infantry or cavalry, and they included troops with specialist skills. They had an important role to play in battle, often joining the legionaries at the forefront of the fighting.

CAVALRY

Every Roman legion included a small number of cavalry, but auxiliaries provided most of the cavalry in the Roman army. They were recruited from tribes around the empire that were skilled in horsemanship.

SHIELD

Auxiliary cavalry carried flat shields that were oval, rectangular, or hexagonal.

SPECIAL FORCES

Unlike legionaries, auxiliaries were not Roman citizens. They were soldiers recruited from the lands that Rome had conquered. They helped to defend the empire's borders and brought a range of different fighting skills to the battlefield. After 25 years of service, they were rewarded with the prize of citizenship.

ARCHERS
The best Roman archers came from Crete and Syria. They used bows made from layers of sinew, wood, and horn glued together.

ARMOR
Auxiliaries often wore chain mail shirts over a tunic. Their helmets were similar to those of legionaries.

COMBAT STATS

Auxiliary forces
The Roman imperial army included around 200,000 auxiliaries. They were divided into units containing:

- **Cavalry:** 40 troops of horsemen, each with 32 men (40 x 32 = 1,280 soldiers)
- **Infantry:** 16 centuries, each with 80 men (16 x 80 = 1,280 men)
- **Mixed forces:** 6 centuries of 80 infantry (6 x 80 = 480 men) working with 4 cavalry troops

FIGHTING AS A UNIT

Roman armies won battles because they fought together as units of highly trained soldiers working in **formation**. They used a range of battle tactics, depending on the circumstances. Careful planning, flexibility, and discipline were key to their success.

BATTLE LINES

In battle, legionaries moved forward in lines. Their shields formed a defensive wall against oncoming weapons. When soldiers in the front line became exhausted, they moved back, and soldiers in the line behind took their place.

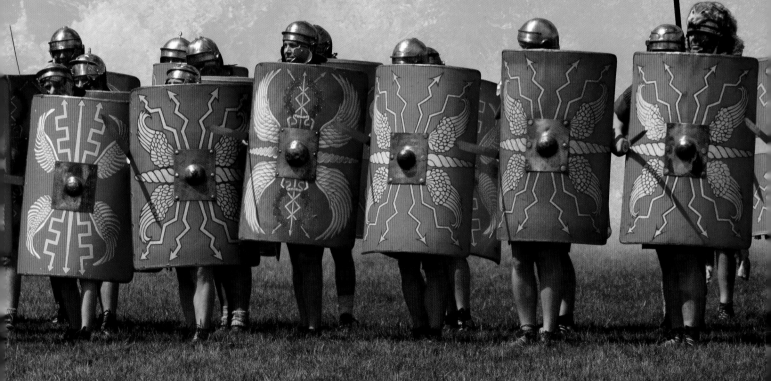

TESTUDO FORMATION

The tortoise, or *testudo*, formation was used for attacking forts or against mounted archers. The soldiers at the front interlocked their upright shields. The soldiers behind raised their shields above their heads to form a protective "shell." This shell was so strong that, during training, a chariot could be driven across the top.

FIGHTING TALK

Battlefield commands

ad aciem: form battle line (ranks facing the enemy)

pila iacite: throw javelins

cuneum facite: form a wedge (an attack formation to break enemy lines)

gladios stringite: draw swords

parate: get ready to charge

percutite: charge

testudinem facite: form *testudo*

FIREPOWER

As well as swords and spears, Roman warriors used heavy weapons, or artillery, on the battlefield, including catapults that fired a range of devastating missiles. When they attacked an enemy fortress or city, Roman soldiers used catapults and ballistas, supported by **battering rams** and high **siege towers**.

DEADLY ONAGER

The most fearsome and powerful Roman catapult was the onager. It got its name from a type of wild ass (the onager) because of the way it kicked when fired.

SLING

A sling attached to the firing arm held the missiles, perhaps one large rock or a barrage of smaller stones.

FIRING ARM

A long wooden arm was fastened with thick, twisted ropes that acted like springs. Soldiers pulled back the arm with a **winch**, twisting the ropes tighter. When the arm was released, it shot forward, firing rocks to smash through stone walls.

WAR MACHINES

Every Roman legion was equipped with a variety of powerful artillery weapons. The artillery men were called *ballistarii*—and they dreaded wet weather. If rain soaked the ropes that gave the catapults their tension, or power, they were useless.

ANCIENT BALLISTA

The ballista was like a giant crossbow. Two soldiers turned winch wheels to pull the arms back and fire huge arrows at the enemy.

SCORPIO

The scorpio was a lethal weapon of great precision and power. It was designed to give a clear view of the target. It fired **bolts** that could pierce through armor and kill a man at a distance of 110 yards (100 m).

COMBAT STATS

Legionary firepower

- **Onager:** 10 in each legion; hurled rocks weighing up to 150 pounds (70 kg)
- **Ballista:** 20 in each legion; range 300-550 yards (275-500 m); speed of missile 115 mph (184 km/h)
- **Scorpio:** 60 in each legion; range up to 440 yards (400 m); firing rate of up to 3-4 bolts per minute

MAKING CAMP

On **campaign**, Roman soldiers spent many days on the march. At the end of each day, they set up well-organized camps, heavily defended by ditches and lines of sharpened stakes. Tents were set up in rows—one for each squad of eight men.

MESSMATES

Recruits lived in eight-man squads called *contubernia*. A legionary's *contubernium* became like his family. The soldiers ate, slept, and trained together, and fought next to one another in battle.

HEAVY EQUIPMENT

The heavy equipment needed in camp was carried by mules. This included tents and large cooking pots, as well as grindstones for making flour from the grain rations.

CAMP ORGANIZATION

Roman legionaries would march for around five hours a day and then stop to make camp. They were experts at setting up camp quickly and efficiently, with each soldier having specific duties. Camps varied in size, but they all had the same basic layout.

COMMANDER IN CAMP

Centurions were responsible for discipline in camp. Punishments included giving soldiers rations of hated barley instead of wheat. For serious offenses, such as running away in battle, a soldier faced *fustuarium*— being beaten to death by the men whose lives he had put at risk.

TENT

The tents in this reconstructed Roman camp are made from canvas, but Roman warriors slept in tents that were usually made from calf or goat skin.

FIGHTING TALK

Rations

The Roman army didn't provide meals but issued rations, with each squad cooking their own food. Legionaries were given a daily grain ration of 3 pounds 5 ounces (1.5 kg). The main ration was wheat grain, made into bread or a type of porridge called *puls*. *Puls* was made with grain, water, salt, and oil or milk. Spices, vegetables, or bacon could be added.

FORTS AND FRONTIERS

Roman legions were not just fighting forces. Part of the job of the army was to build permanent forts and lines of defense on the borders of the empire. Legions included architects and engineers, and many soldiers were skilled craftsmen, such as stonemasons and carpenters.

CONSTRUCTION TEAM

When the Romans conquered new territory, they then had to defend it. Roman soldiers dug defensive ditches along the frontiers of the empire, as well as forts surrounded by **ramparts**.

FRONTIER DEFENDERS

The most important frontier in the empire was the Limes Germanicus. This was in Europe, along the Rhine and Danube rivers. It divided the Roman Empire from Germanic tribes. The frontier stretched for 353 miles (568 km), and there were 60 forts and 900 watchtowers along its length. Fifteen legions were stationed there.

PATROLLING HADRIAN'S WALL

The best surviving frontier is Hadrian's Wall in Britain. The mighty wall formed the northern frontier between Roman Britain and Scotland. It was guarded and patrolled by auxiliary forces for almost 250 years.

COMBAT STATS

Hadrian's Wall

- **Built:** 122–128 CE by Emperor Hadrian
- **Length:** 73 miles (118 km)
- **Height:** about 15 feet (4.5 m)
- **Thickness:** up to 10 feet (3 m)
- **Forts:** 16 large forts along the wall, each housing between 500 and 1,000 men; 79 small forts at intervals of 5,000 feet (1,500 m)

THE SACRED EAGLE

One of the most important roles in a Roman legion was that of the *aquilifer*, who carried the legion's eagle standard. The eagle was a sacred **emblem**, held high on a pole in battle so everyone could see it. It was the legion's most treasured possession, and legionaries would die to protect it from capture.

AQUILA
Every legion had an eagle standard (*aquila*), displaying an eagle with outstretched wings. If the *aquila* fell into enemy hands during battle, it brought disgrace on the legion.

SPQR
The letters "SPQR" stood for *senatus populusque Romanus* ("the senate and people of Rome")—the Roman state, for which the legions were fighting.

ARMY COMMANDER
Standards often showed an image of the reigning emperor, the commander of the Roman army. This standard of the 10th Legion depicts the Emperor Tiberius (ruled 14–37 CE).

RALLYING POINT

On the march, the *aquilifer* carried the eagle standard at the front. Each century also had a standard, called a *signum*. Carried by the *signifer*, this tall standard was an important rallying point for soldiers during battle.

SIGNUM
Each century had its own unique standard, the *signum*, carried by the *signifer*.

METAL DISKS
A century's *signum* displayed up to six metal disks. The number of disks may have indicated the number of the century within the cohort to which it belonged.

BATTLE REPORT

The Battle of Carrhae, 53 BCE

At the Battle of Carrhae, in the Province of Syria (modern Turkey), Parthian horse archers and cavalry completely defeated seven Roman legions led by General Marcus Crassus. The legionary standards were captured, and Rome was shamed. The standards were kept by the Parthians for 33 years, until Emperor Augustus negotiated their return in 20 BCE. This was seen as one of the great achievements of Augustus.

THE GREATEST COMMANDER

Rome had many great military commanders, but most historians agree that the most brilliant Roman general was Gaius Julius Caesar. With his vast army, Caesar conquered Gaul in 58–50 BCE and invaded Britain twice, in 55 and 54 BCE.

HAIL CAESAR!
Julius Caesar (played here by Timothy Dalton in the movie *Cleopatra*) was a popular and powerful general. He became dictator, or sole ruler, of the Roman Empire, before being assassinated by his enemies in Rome, in 44 BCE.

SUCCESS IN GAUL

Julius Caesar led the Roman army to victory in many great battles. One of his greatest successes was the siege of the huge hill fort of Alesia in Gaul, in 52 BCE. After a seven-year campaign, Gaul had finally been conquered.

ENCLOSING WALL

Caesar ordered his men to surround Alesia with wooden fortifications, which enclosed the Gauls in the hill fort and cut off their supplies. He hoped to starve the Gauls into surrender.

WATCHTOWER

Every 80 feet (24 m) along the walls, the Romans built a watchtower fitted with ballistas.

BATTLE REPORT

Siege of Alesia, 52 BCE

The siege of Alesia is considered a classic example of siege tactics and one of Caesar's greatest military achievements. Caesar's men built a line of fortifications 11 miles (8 km) long to trap 80,000 Gauls inside the hill fort. They then constructed another set 13 miles (22 km) long to keep out a relieving army of 60,000 soldiers. In the final battle, Caesar's army of 40,000 was close to defeat when Caesar led a surprise cavalry attack against the rear of the enemy's relief force. The retreating Gallic warriors were slaughtered or captured, and every Roman soldier was given a prisoner as a slave.

END OF EMPIRE

By the end of the third century CE, the mighty Roman Empire had split into two parts—the Western Empire, with its capital in Rome, and the Eastern Empire, with its capital in Byzantium, today's Istanbul. The empire in the East remained strong, but the Western Empire was crumbling. Its defenses had become weak, and soon it was overrun by invaders.

FACING INVASION

By the third century CE, the Roman Empire was suffering wave after wave of **barbarian** invasions. Facing continual attacks on its borders, the once **invincible** Roman legions began to lose control.

FIGHTING TALK

Romans vs. Goths

In 378 CE, Emperor Valens fought an army of **Goths** at Adrianople in modern Turkey. The Goths were a barbarian people who had been allowed to settle in the empire as allies, but rebelled when they were mistreated. Valens' army of around 20,000, mostly legionary infantry, was wiped out by Goth cavalry. The battle signaled the beginning of the collapse of the Western Roman Empire.

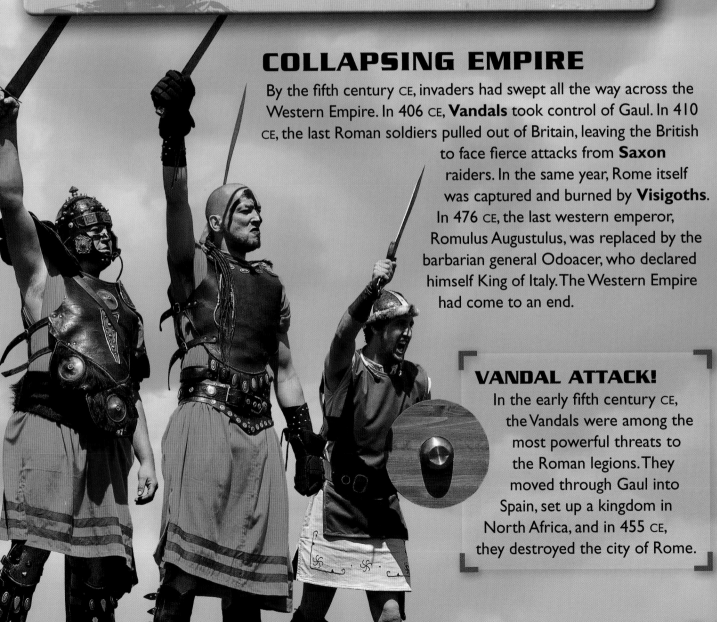

COLLAPSING EMPIRE

By the fifth century CE, invaders had swept all the way across the Western Empire. In 406 CE, **Vandals** took control of Gaul. In 410 CE, the last Roman soldiers pulled out of Britain, leaving the British to face fierce attacks from **Saxon** raiders. In the same year, Rome itself was captured and burned by **Visigoths**. In 476 CE, the last western emperor, Romulus Augustulus, was replaced by the barbarian general Odoacer, who declared himself King of Italy. The Western Empire had come to an end.

VANDAL ATTACK!

In the early fifth century CE, the Vandals were among the most powerful threats to the Roman legions. They moved through Gaul into Spain, set up a kingdom in North Africa, and in 455 CE, they destroyed the city of Rome.

GLOSSARY

auxiliary a soldier who provided support to the Roman legions

ballista a heavy weapon like a giant crossbow

barbarian a Roman word for non-Romans (literally "bearded ones")

battering ram a heavy beam used to smash down walls

bolt a short, heavy arrow

campaign a military operation in a particular area

centurion a commander of a century in the Roman army

century a unit of 80 men (originally 100) in the Roman army; the centuries in the first cohort were double-strength, with 160 men

citizen in Rome, a man entitled to vote in elections and serve in the legions

cohort a unit in the Roman army consisting of six centuries (except the first cohort in each legion, which consisted of five double-strength centuries)

denarius a Roman coin (plural *denarii*)

emblem a symbol

emperor the ruler of an empire

empire a country or state and all the lands it controls

formation in battle, the way soldiers are arranged

frontier the border at the edge of a country or empire

Gaul the Roman province that covered France, Belgium, and the Rhine region of Germany

Goth a member of a Germanic people that invaded the Roman Empire

imperial relating to an empire

invincible unbeatable

legionary a soldier serving in a Roman legion

noble a person belonging to the aristocratic class

rampart a mound of earth raised to fortify a place

reserves soldiers outside the front line who were held back in case they were needed

Saxon a member of a Germanic people that conquered parts of Britain

senator an official in the Roman government

siege a military operation in which forces try to capture a fortress, town, or city

standard a military symbol, like a flag

tactic the way a plan, such as a battle plan, is performed

Vandal a member of a Germanic people that invaded Rome, Gaul, Spain, and North Africa

Visigoth a member of a branch of the Goths

winch a crank or handle

FURTHER INFORMATION

Books

Ancient Rome by Simon James (Dorling Kindersley, 2008)

Gladiators and Roman Soldiers by Charlotte Guillain (Raintree, 2011)

How to Be a Roman Soldier by Fiona MacDonald (National Geographic, 2008)

An Illustrated Encyclopedia of the Uniforms of the Roman World: A Detailed Study of the Armies of Rome and Their Enemies by Kevin F. Kiley (Lorenz Books, 2013)

Navigators: Ancient Rome by Philip Steele and Steve Stone (Kingfisher, 2012)

The Romans (Illustrated World History) by Anthony Marks and Graham Tingay (Usborne Books, 2010)

Web Sites

Ancient Rome

www.historyforkids.org/learn/romans/

Find out surprising facts about the Roman Empire. This amazing portal has links to photos, maps, and features about all aspects of Roman culture, from the history of its many wars and military leaders, to daily life, religion, games, and its spectacular architecture.

Ermine Street Guard

www.erminestreetguard.co.uk/

The informative web site of one of the oldest Roman reenactment groups in the world, famous for recreating and testing Roman weapons and equipment. Includes photos of authentic military uniforms and artillery.

The Roman Empire in the First Century

www.pbs.org/empires/romans/

An awesome and educational web site based on the PBS television series, packed with features including a war timeline, family tree of Roman leaders, virtual library with excerpts from real Roman authors, games, quizzes, and more.

Index